Contents

The game of basketball

The first game of basketball was played in the US in December 1891. A sports teacher thought up the game to keep his students active indoors during the winter months. Peach baskets were used as the first basketball goals. Now it is one of world's most popular sports and has been played in the Olympic Games since 1936.

In schools, players under the age of 12 play a version of the game called Mini-Basketball. This book covers the rules and way of playing Mini-Basketball.

STARTING SPORT

Basketball

Rebecca Hunter

Photography by Chris Fairclough

FRANKLIN WATTS

First published in 2009 by
Franklin Watts
338 Euston Road
London NW1 3BH

Franklin Watts Australia
Level 17/207 Kent Street
Sydney NSW 2000

ISBN: 978 0 7496 8944 5

Dewey classification number: 796.323

A CIP catalogue record for this book is available from the British Library.

Planning and production by Discovery Books Limited
Editor: Rebecca Hunter
Designer: Ian Winton
Illustrator: Stefan Chabluk
Photography: Chris Fairclough
Additional photography: Gettyimages p. 21 bottom Fernando Medina/NBAE,
p. 27 Feng Li.

Consultant: Martin Spencer, Mini-Basketball England Education Officer.

The author, packager and publisher would like to thank the following people
for their participation in this book: Helen Fogden and the students of
Northampton Academy and Weston Favell School.

Printed in China

Franklin Watts is a division of Hachette Children's Books,
an Hachette UK company.
www.hachette.co.uk

Kit

Wear comfortable, loose-fitting clothes for basketball as you need to be able to move around the court easily. Players usually wear baggy shorts and a vest. The vests are numbered 4 to 15. You may need a sweat-shirt to keep warm when not playing.

Shoes

Wearing good basketball shoes is also very important as the game puts a big strain on the ankle joints.

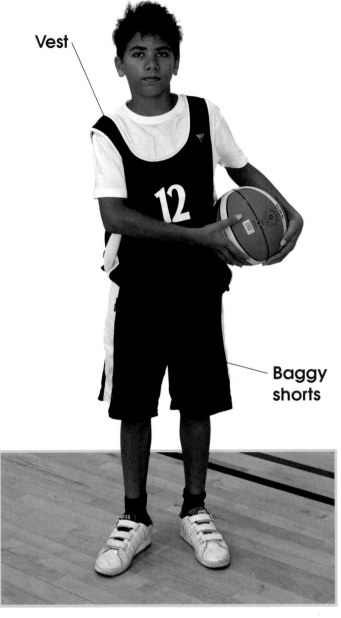

Vest

Baggy shorts

Shoes can have high or low ankle supports. Wear whatever is comfortable for you but make sure the soles are clean and that your laces, if you have them, are always tied up correctly.

7

The court and positions

A basketball court can be outside, although many are indoors. A full-sized court is 22m x 12m but they can be smaller. At each end of the court are the goals, which are a basket consisting of a hoop and net. Behind the basket is the backboard, which helps direct the ball into the net.

In the centre of the court is the centre circle. This is where play starts. Under the basket is an area called the zone, key or restricted area. It is called a restricted area because when a team is on the attack, none of the team can stay in this area for longer than 3 seconds.

Backboard

Basket

Centre circle

Restricted area

Endline

4.00m

Sideline

Free-throw line

The ball is usually made of rubber or **synthetic** leather and should be size 5 or 6 depending on the age of the players.

Teams

A complete Mini-Basketball team consists of 10 players but only five can be on court at any one time. Five **substitutes** sit on the bench and can be used for substitution during the game period.

Positions

All players can go anywhere on the court. However, so that players know where they should be and play a good game, there are three playing positions.

Guards are usually the smallest and fastest members of the team.

Forwards are taller than the guards and good at scoring goals from the side of the court.

The **centre** is usually the tallest player and is good at catching rebounds and scoring close to the basket.

The aim of the game is to score more points than the opposition by scoring baskets. The number of points scored depends on the position from which the player scores the basket (see page 20).

Rules of the game

The game is divided into two halves of twenty minutes each, with an interval of ten minutes between them. Each half is divided into two periods of ten minutes. Players can be substituted between each period. Each player must play in two periods – unless they have been injured, **disqualified** or have committed five **fouls**.

Basketball has many rules. These are the most basic ones you need to know to play a game. If you break any of these rules the referee will blow the whistle and make a sign to show which rule has been broken.

Travelling rule: You cannot walk or run while holding the ball (below right). To move on court you must **dribble**.

Illegal dribble: A player is not allowed to dribble the ball with two hands at the same time, or let the ball come to rest in the hands and then continue to dribble. This is often called a double dribble.

Throw-ins

When a rule is broken, the ball is given to the opponents for a throw-in from out-of-bounds at the place nearest to where the foul took place.

Three-second rule: A player shall not remain in the opponents' restricted area for more than three seconds whilst his or her team is in control of the ball.

Player-out-of-bounds and ball out-of-bounds: Both the players and the ball must stay inside the playing area. A player or ball are out-of-bounds when they touch the boundary line or anything outside the boundary line.

Fouls

If you touch another player unfairly (e.g. by pushing or shoving them) this is called a personal foul. Showing unsportsmanlike behaviour is also a foul. A player who commits five fouls during the game must leave the game immediately and be replaced by a substitute.

Warming up

Basketball is an **energetic** sport. You need to warm up well before playing to reduce the risk of hurting yourself and to be fit and ready for the game.

Jogging

Begin with at least five minutes jogging to increase your heart rate and get your blood pumping.

Stretches

Step forward and stretch the back of one leg. Then step forward again stretching the back of the other leg. Continue this action across the court.

Arm exercises

Light circling of the arms, forwards and backwards, will warm up the shoulder muscles. Take your arms across to one side and then the other, gently twisting the top half of the body to each side. Prepare for jumping in the game by doing some jumping movements.

Ball handling

When you are fully warmed and stretched, practise some ball-handling skills. You could do some dribbling or passing of the ball to a friend. You could also take some practice shots at the basket. These can be combined in a team warm-up where you take turns in dribbling, shooting and collecting the ball after the shot or rebound.

Playing a game

Play starts with a **jump ball**. One player from each team stands in the centre circle. The referee then tosses the ball up between them.

Both players jump up and try and tap the ball, but only after it has reached its highest point. All the other players remain outside the circle until the ball has been tapped. They then move to catch the ball.

Formation

Once the ball is in play, the team in possession of the ball attempts to move into a shooting position. Teams can move into a **formation** on court in order to attack the basket. One formation that is often used is the 2-1-2 formation with the players spread evenly around the attacking basket.

This allows the team to spread out to play 'give and go'. This is where a player receives the ball then passes it to a team mate and moves into a new position.

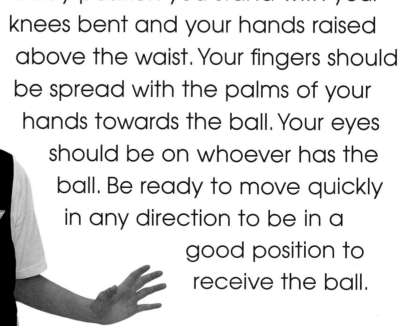

The ready position

When you do not have the ball you need to keep yourself ready for anything. In the ready position you stand with your knees bent and your hands raised above the waist. Your fingers should be spread with the palms of your hands towards the ball. Your eyes should be on whoever has the ball. Be ready to move quickly in any direction to be in a good position to receive the ball.

Dribbling

In basketball the ball can be moved about court in two ways: by passing the ball or by dribbling.

When dribbling, you must touch the ball with all five fingers and not the palm of your hand. You may only use one hand at a time, but you can change hands as often as you like. This is called a cross-over dribble.

How to dribble

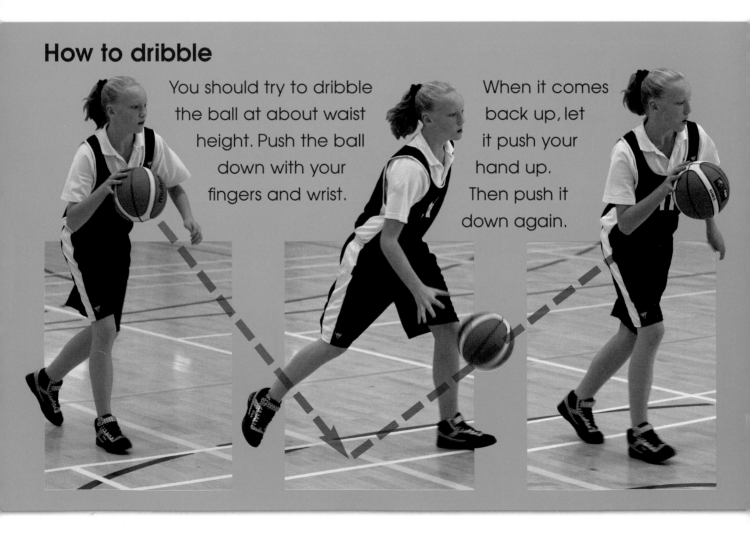

You should try to dribble the ball at about waist height. Push the ball down with your fingers and wrist.

When it comes back up, let it push your hand up. Then push it down again.

The pivot

While dribbling, you may change direction by pivoting. The pivot is a way of changing direction while keeping one foot on ground.

When you come to a stop with the ball, keep one foot on the ground and step with the other one. You may pivot in any direction.

Dribbling drills

Lay out a maze of cones on the ground and practise dribbling the ball in and out of them. Try timing yourself and give yourself faults if you touch the cones!

Passing

Passing the ball is a much faster way of moving it than dribbling.

Chest pass

The chest pass (right) is used when there is no-one between you and the person you are passing to. Look at the player to whom you are going to pass. Hold the ball in both hands. Step forward and keeping your elbows in, push the ball towards the **receiver**. Release it by extending your arms and fingers.

Bounce pass

Start in a similar position to the chest pass but bounce the ball to the receiver. The ball must hit the floor in just the correct position on the floor to be successful. This might be just under the arms of a **defender**. You can make a bounce pass using two or just one hand.

Overhead Pass

If you want to pass the ball over the defenders, use an overhead pass. Your arms should be raised above your head (but not behind). Aim the ball into the raised hands of the receiver.

Receiving

If you do not have the ball, you should be ready to receive it at any time. Watch the person who has the ball and try to get into a free space. Show them you are ready to receive the ball by showing with your hands where you want to receive it. When the ball is passed to you, move forward to catch it.

Passing activities

With a partner pass the ball between you using a different type of pass each time. Using two balls, try passing at the same time. One ball will have to go higher or to one side so the balls do not meet.

Shooting

All players can score baskets. When you score a basket during active play it is worth 2 points. A basket scored during a **free throw** is worth 1 point.

Set shot

A set shot is a shot scored from a standing position. You should be standing with your knees slightly bent with the ball held in front of your chest. As you straighten your legs, push the ball up towards the basket. Release the ball with a flick of your wrists so that it drops into the basket.

Lay-up shot

A lay-up shot is made when you are dribbling towards the basket and scoring on the move. You should jump off the opposite foot to your shooting hand. Jump as high as you can, releasing the ball when you are at full stretch and holding the ball as high as possible. Aim the ball at the backboard so it rebounds into the basket.

Slam dunk

The slam dunk is a spectacular shot to watch, but difficult to perform. The player jumps so high that they can push the ball down into the basket. You need to be very tall or a very good jumper to do this shot!

Defending

Defence is all about stopping the attacking team getting into a scoring position. The defence stance is almost the same as the ready position. The arms should be out to the side with hands up, fingers spread. You should be well balanced on the balls of your feet, ready to move in any direction. Shuffle your feet along the floor to move quickly.

One-on-one defence

When defending, each player is assigned to mark one other player on the opposing team. Stay between the person you are marking and the basket at all times. Be ready to **intercept** the ball if it is passed to your player but do not be caught out of position by going for the ball.

Defending against a dribbler

Always keep between the player and the basket. Keep your hands down near the ball. Stay an arm's length from your opponent. Look for an opportunity to flick the ball away from them. Keep moving into the position that the dribbler wants to go.

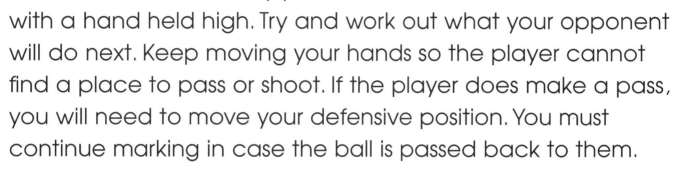

Defending against a passer or shooter

Stand in the basic ready position with a hand held high. Try and work out what your opponent will do next. Keep moving your hands so the player cannot find a place to pass or shoot. If the player does make a pass, you will need to move your defensive position. You must continue marking in case the ball is passed back to them.

Defending activity

Get a friend to dribble the ball in a zig-zag across the court towards the basket. Practise your defensive moves by trying to stay between them and the basket. Try to intercept the ball, but be careful not to touch them.

Rebound play

When the ball misses the basket it often bounces back off the backboard. Either team can then catch it. Catching the ball after a rebound is an important skill to learn.

There are two types of **rebound play**. In an offensive rebound the attacking team gets the ball back. A defensive rebound is where the defending team gains possession of the ball.

Offensive rebounds

You must be ready for every shot your team takes and watch carefully where the ball is shot from. Anticipate where the rebound will go and move quickly to catch it. When you get the ball, immediately jump up and shoot for the basket.

Defensive rebounds

When an opposing player shoots, turn your back on them and try to be in a position to jump for the ball as it rebounds. Avoid getting too far underneath the basket. If you get the ball, move it out of the key area as quickly as possible.

Free throws

Free throws are given when a player is fouled while in the act of shooting. The player fouled is given two free shots from the free-throw line. Three defenders and two attackers line up along the sides of the zone. They may not enter the restricted area to catch the rebound until the ball has left the hands of the free-throw shooter. No player may touch the ball until it has touched the ring.

Other ways to play

Take Six Mini-Basketball

Take Six Mini-Basketball is a popular version of the game for younger players. There are six players in a team, three are on the court at any time. Each player gets a chance to play in every position. Substitutes help with the game by keeping score, timekeeping and assisting the referee.

Adult basketball

When you reach secondary school you will start to play the adult version of basketball. You will play on a bigger court, with a higher basket and a larger ball. There will be some more rules to learn. You will not necessarily play an equal proportion of the game as the other players. The coach can decide which players to substitute and for how long.

Wheelchair basketball

Disabled soldiers first played wheelchair basketball in the US in the 1940s. Now it is played all over the world by thousands of athletes. In some countries, able-bodied athletes are allowed to play the game too.

Glossary

defender a player who is marking an opponent with or without the ball

disqualified to be removed from the rest of the game

dribbling standing or moving while bouncing the ball with one hand

energetic involving great activity

formation an agreed set of positions

foul when a player makes physical contact with an opponent unfairly

free throw an unopposed attempt to score a goal from the free-throw line

intercept to gain possession of the ball when passed or dribbled by an opponent

jump ball throwing up the ball between two opposing players to start play

rebound play the act of catching the ball after a missed shot rebounds off the backboard

receiver a person waiting to receive the ball

substitutes players who are waiting to replace members of the team already playing on court

synthetic something made from chemical, not natural, materials

Further reading

Basketball: Tell Me About Sport, Clive Gifford, Evans Brothers Ltd, 2009

Basketball: Know Your Sport, Clive Gifford, Franklin Watts, 2008

Learning Basketball, Katrin Barth and Lothar Boesing, Meyer & Meyer Sports Books, 2008

Basketball Fun and Games, Keven Prusak, Human Kinetics Europe Ltd, 2005

How to Improve at Basketball, Jim Drewett, Ticktock Media Ltd, 2005

Further information

England Basketball
PO Box 3971
Sheffield
S9 9AZ
Website: www.englandbasketball.com

Basketball Australia
PO Box 7141
Alexandria
NSW 2015
Website: www.basketball.net.au

Mini-Basketball
4 Fairmead Rise
Northampton
NN2 8PP
Website: www.mini-basketball.org.uk

Australian Sports Commission
PO Box 176
Belconnen
ACT 2616
Website: www.ausport.gov.au

Index